Archangels For Kids

Written By: Melanie Lynn Pederson

Illustrated By: Camilla Marie Phillips

For Molly, Wyatt,

and Camilla.

I love you tons!

Companion Coloring Book Available at

www.MelanieLynnPederson.com

Parents interested in Archangels - check out

Invoking the Archangels by Sunny Dawn Johnston

ISBN 13: 978-0692629628

ISBN 10: 0692629629

There are seven Archangels. Michael (MY-kle), Gabriel (GAY-bree-el), Chamuel (SHAM-you-el, Jophiel (JOE-fee-el), Raphael (RAPH-eye-el), Zadkiel (ZAD-key-el, and Uriel (YUR-ee-el).

The Archangels are with you and showering you with love all the time. The Archangels are waiting to help and comfort you whenever you ask. Each Archangel has their own special color and gift to share.

How to Connect with Archangels

1. Say "Angels, please help me."
   Angels only help when asked

2. Give them permission to help
   Say "I am open to your help."

3. Believe they will help you
   Sometimes you have to wait

4. Receive their messages and help
   Songs, color, feelings, coins, etc

Archangel Michael

(MY-kle)

His color is blue. He is the Archangel of protection, guidance, and strength. Archangel Michael helps with feeling good about yourself, gaining courage, and getting rid of fear.

Call on Archangel Michael when you don't feel safe. Imagine you are surrounded in a big blue bubble to protect you. You can also imagine holding a big blue shield. Wear blue when you want to feel close to Archangel Michael.

Archangel Gabriel

(GAY-bree-el)

His color is white. He is the archangel of talking. Archangel Gabriel helps with telling someone how you feel or when you need help with writing.

Call on Archangel Gabriel
when you need to tell the
truth. Imagine white light
coming down from the sky
surrounding you in warm
white love. Wear white
when you want to feel
close to Archangel
Gabriel.

Archangel Chamuel
(SHAM-you-el)

His color is pink. He is

the archangel of

unconditional love.

Archangel Chamuel helps

with loving yourself, loving

others, and finding things

that are lost.

Call on Archangel Chamuel when you are lonely, sad, or need to find something. Imagine you are wrapped up in a big, fluffy, warm pink blanket. Feel his love on our skin and in your heart. Wear pink when you want to feel close to Archangel Chamuel.

Archangel Jophiel

(JOE-fee-el)

His color is yellow. He is the archangel of creativity, beauty, and art. Archangel Jophiel helps with feeling hope, joy, and seeing the good in the world.

Call on Archangel Jophiel when you don't feel good about yourself, are working on an art project, or when you have sad thoughts. Imagine bright yellow light coming down from the sky surrounding you. Wear yellow when you want to feel close to Archangel Jophiel.

Archangel Raphael

(RAF-eye-el)

His color is green. He is the archangel of healing your body and your feelings. Archangel Raphael helps with finding lost pets, healing booboos, and fixing hurt feelings.

Call on Archangel Raphael when you get hurt, someone says something mean to you, or you need help with a decision. Imagine you are surrounded by a bubble of green light. Wear green when you want to feel close to Archangel Raphael.

Archangel Zadkiel

(ZAD-key-el)

His color is purple. He is the archangel of forgiveness, kindness, and sympathy. Archangel Zadkiel helps with remembering things, forgiving yourself, and forgiving others.

Call on Archangel Zadkiel when you've hurt someone or someone has hurt you. Imagine a purple fire on top of your head. Feel all your yucky thoughts and yucky feelings burn up in the purple fire. Wear purple when you want to feel close to Archangel Zadkiel.

Archangel Uriel

(UR-ee-el)

His color is red. He is the
archangel of new ideas
and making changes.
Archangel Uriel helps with
learning, fixing problems,
and peace.

Call on Archangel Uriel when you aren't sure what to do, are having trouble at school, or are confused. Imagine your whole body surrounded by a big red bubble. Wear red when you want to feel close to Archangel Uriel.

Parents, you can learn more about the Archangels in an adult format! Check out

Invoking the Archangels by Sunny Dawn Johnston

Made in the USA
Middletown, DE
25 September 2022